EXPLORING COUNTRIES

The Philippines

by Derek Zobel

BLASTOFF!
READERS
5

BELLWETHER MEDIA · MINNEAPOLIS, MN

Note to Librarians, Teachers, and Parents:

Blastoff! Readers are carefully developed by literacy experts and combine standards-based content with developmentally appropriate text.

Level 1 provides the most support through repetition of high-frequency words, light text, predictable sentence patterns, and strong visual support.

Level 2 offers early readers a bit more challenge through varied simple sentences, increased text load, and less repetition of high-frequency words.

Level 3 advances early-fluent readers toward fluency through increased text and concept load, less reliance on visuals, longer sentences, and more literary language.

Level 4 builds reading stamina by providing more text per page, increased use of punctuation, greater variation in sentence patterns, and increasingly challenging vocabulary.

Level 5 encourages children to move from "learning to read" to "reading to learn" by providing even more text, varied writing styles, and less familiar topics.

Whichever book is right for your reader, Blastoff! Readers are the perfect books to build confidence and encourage a love of reading that will last a lifetime!

This edition first published in 2012 by Bellwether Media, Inc.

No part of this publication may be reproduced in whole or in part without written permission of the publisher. For information regarding permission, write to Bellwether Media, Inc., Attention: Permissions Department, 5357 Penn Avenue South, Minneapolis, MN 55419.

Library of Congress Cataloging-in-Publication Data
Zobel, Derek, 1983-
 The Philippines / by Derek Zobel.
    p. cm. – (Blastoff! readers: exploring countries)
 Summary: "Developed by literacy experts for students in grades three through seven, this book introduces young readers to the geography and culture of the Philippines"–Provided by publisher.
 Includes bibliographical references and index.
 ISBN 978-1-60014-622-0 (hardcover : alk. paper)
 1. Philippines-Juvenile literature. I. Title.
DS655.Z63 2012
959.9–dc22   2011005685

Printed in the United States of America, North Mankato, MN.

080111   1187

Contents

Where Is the Philippines?   4
The Land   6
The Pacific Ring of Fire   8
Wildlife   10
The People   12
Daily Life   14
Going to School   16
Working   18
Playing   20
Food   22
Holidays   24
Rizal Park   26
Fast Facts   28
Glossary   30
To Learn More   31
Index   32

Taiwan

South
China
Sea

Pacific
Ocean

Luzon

Manila

The
Philippines

Visayas

Sulu
Sea

Mindanao

Malaysia

Celebes
Sea

4

Indonesia

Philippine Sea

The Philippines is a group of islands located in Southeast Asia. More than 7,100 islands make up the **archipelago**. In total, the country covers 115,831 square miles (300,000 square kilometers). The two largest islands are Luzon in the north and Mindanao in the southeast. An island group called the Visayas sits between these islands. Manila, the country's capital, is located on the western coast of Luzon.

The Philippines does not border any other countries. Its closest neighbors are Malaysia, Taiwan, and Indonesia. The Sulu Sea and the Celebes Sea lie to the south. To the north lies the South China Sea. The Philippine Sea and the Pacific Ocean lie to the east.

The Philippines has mountains, hills, plains, and sandy beaches. Mountain ranges are more common on the larger islands. Mount Apo, the country's highest peak, sits on the island of Mindanao. It towers 9,692 feet (2,954 meters) over the surrounding land.

Most of the Philippines is covered in **tropical rain forests**. The Cagayan, the Agusan, and other rivers flow down from the mountains. They feed the rain forests and the country's **fertile** plains on their way to the sea. Along the coasts, bright blue water washes onto white sand. **Coral reefs** lie in the shallow waters off the coasts of many islands.

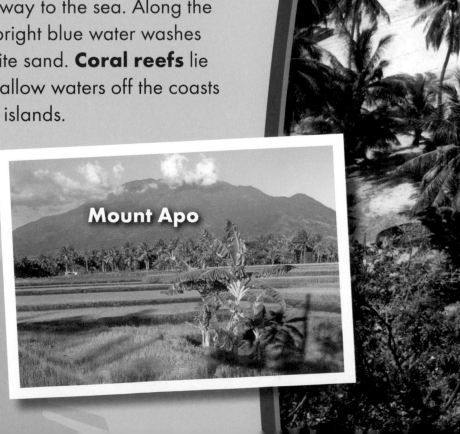

Mount Apo

Did you know?
The Philippine Trench lies in the sea east of the Philippines. The trench is about 820 miles (1,320 kilometers) wide and 34,580 feet (10,540 meters) deep!

fun fact

In 1991, a volcano on Luzon called Mount Pinatubo violently erupted. It destroyed buildings and darkened the sky with ash.

The Philippines is on the western edge of the **Pacific Ring of Fire**. This is an area where earthquakes and **volcanoes** are common because of the movement of Earth's crust. Every day, as many as 20 minor earthquakes shake the Philippines. Off the coasts, earthquakes along the ocean floor sometimes cause **tsunamis**. These giant waves can be over 100 feet (33 meters) high and destroy coastal areas.

Many volcanoes erupt in the Philippines. They often puff smoke and spew **lava**. Scientists can usually warn people before a big eruption. This gives people enough time to move to a safe place.

Did you know?
Mount Mayon is one of the most active volcanoes in the Philippines. Over the last 400 years, it has erupted almost 50 times.

Mount Mayon

Many kinds of wildlife make their homes in the Philippines. Goats, monkeys, deer, and water buffalo are common in the forests and plains. Philippine flying lemurs glide from tree to tree. Tarsiers cling to tree trunks. They use their huge eyes to watch out for pythons, cobras, and other large snakes.

sea horse

tarsier

Philippine eagle

! **fun fact**
The Philippine eagle is the national bird of the Philippines. It has a wingspan of over 6 feet (1.8 meters) and enjoys eating monkeys!

The waters around the Philippines are full of fish, crabs, and many other ocean animals. Along the coasts and in rivers, crocodiles stalk birds and other prey. Sea horses, sea turtles, and tropical fish thrive in the coral reefs off the coasts.

Did you know?

Only the United States and the United Kingdom have more English speakers than the Philippines.

Over 100 million people live in the Philippines. They are called Filipinos. Most have **ancestors** who came from mainland Asia and the islands of Indonesia thousands of years ago. The country has over 100 different people groups. Today, the Tagalog and Cebuano are the largest groups. The Tagalog are found on Luzon and the Cebuano on the Visayas. Many groups speak their own language. Filipino and English are the official languages of the country.

Speak Filipino!

English	Filipino	How to say it
hello	helo	hello
good-bye	paalam	PAH-a-lam
yes	oo	oo
no	hindi	HEEN-dee
please	paki	PAH-kee
thank you	salamat	SAH-lah-maht
friend	kaibigan	KAH-ee-bee-gahn

Did you know?

In both large cities and small villages, Filipinos gather at outdoor markets. They buy, sell, and trade clothing, tools, and food.

Most Filipinos live in cities. In large cities like Manila and Quezon City, people have apartments or small houses. Many people use cars, buses, and motorcycles to get from place to place. Some motorcycles have cabs to carry more than one passenger. Filipinos call these "tricycles."

In the countryside, people live in houses in small villages or on farms. They sometimes ride buses into cities to buy food or other goods. To get from island to island, Filipinos take small airplanes or boats across the sea.

Where People Live in the Philippines

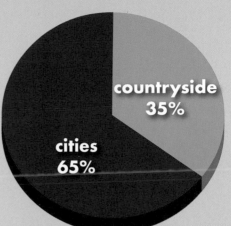

countryside 35%

cities 65%

fun fact

Many Filipinos use jeepneys to get around in cities. These vehicles were made from United States Army Jeeps used during World War II.

jeepney

Children in the Philippines go to elementary school from ages 7 to 12. They learn math, science, English, and Filipino. The government requires children to attend school, but some cannot attend. Many live in areas without schools. Some have no money for books and other supplies.

High school lasts for four years after elementary school. Students focus on history, math, science, and other subjects. After high school, students can go to a university or **vocational school** to prepare for a career.

Working

Where People Work in the Philippines

manufacturing 15%

farming 34%

services 51%

18

The Philippines is rich in **natural resources**. Miners dig into the mountains for gold, copper, and other **minerals**. Out at sea, workers drill into the ocean floor to bring up oil. People **refine** the oil into gasoline and other products. Fishermen catch fish, lobsters, crabs, and many other ocean animals. In the fertile plains along the coasts, farmers grow rice, sugarcane, pineapples, and other crops.

In cities, farmers sell their crops at large markets. Factory workers make electronics, clothing, and other goods that are shipped around the world. Many Filipinos have **service jobs**. They work in restaurants, hotels, schools, and other places that serve people.

sipa

Filipinos enjoy many sports and activities. The two most popular sports are basketball and boxing. *Sipa*, a sport **native** to the Philippines, is played by people of all ages. Players stand on opposite sides of a net and kick a soft ball back and forth. A team scores a point when the other team lets the ball touch the ground.

The landscape of the Philippines allows for many fun outdoor activities. Skiing, **mountaineering**, and rock climbing are popular in the mountains. Along the coasts, people like to swim, scuba dive, and fish.

fun fact

Tinikling is the national dance of the Philippines. Two people tap bamboo poles together and against the ground. One or more dancers jump over and between the poles.

tinikling

Did you know?

For big celebrations, Filipinos often make *lechón*, which is an entire roasted pig.

Dishes that include fish are a specialty of the Philippines. Milkfish, grouper, and tilapia are used in many meals. Filipino food also has Spanish and Asian flavors. Fish, clams, and other seafoods are mixed with rice and vegetables to make *paella*, a Spanish dish. The Spanish introduced garlic to the Philippines. Filipinos add garlic to fried rice to make *sinangag*. It is often eaten for breakfast along with a fried egg and meat. Dishes with chicken and pork include *adobo* and *afritada*. Filipino spring rolls, called *lumpia*, are similar to those made in China. They are stuffed with meat and vegetables. A common dessert enjoyed throughout the country is *halo-halo*. It is a mixture of ice, milk, sugar, coconut, and many kinds of fruits.

halo-halo

paella

Independence Day

Filipinos have many holidays that remember important days in their country's history. On June 12, they celebrate Independence Day. This marks the day when the Philippines became free from Spanish control. Filipinos also celebrate their independence from the United States on July 4. National Heroes' Day occurs on the last Monday in August. It honors Filipinos who fought hard for their country's freedom.

Most Filipinos are **Catholic** and celebrate Christian holidays such as Easter and Christmas. From December 16 to Christmas, many Catholic Filipinos go to an early church service every day. Some services start as early as 4 o'clock in the morning!

Did you know?

On December 30, Filipinos remember José Rizal's life and work with Rizal Day.

Rizal Park is located in the center of Manila. Near the end of the 1800s, it was the location of many famous events in the Philippine **Revolution**. It is named after José Rizal, a man who died fighting the Spanish for the country's independence.

A **monument** to Rizal and other heroes from the revolution stands in the park. Today, the park has become a daily gathering place for Filipinos. It is a place where people picnic, play, and celebrate. They enjoy the freedom that their ancestors fought hard to win for their country.

fun fact

The Quirino Grandstand is located in Rizal Park. It is the traditional place where newly elected presidents are sworn into office.

Fast Facts About the Philippines

The Philippines' Flag

The flag of the Philippines has a blue stripe on the top and a red stripe on the bottom. The blue stands for justice, peace, and truth. The red stands for courage and honor. On the left side is a white triangle that contains a gold sun and three gold stars. It represents liberty. The flag was officially adopted on June 12, 1898.

Official Name: Republic of the Philippines

Area: 115,831 square miles (300,000 square kilometers); the Philippines is the 72nd largest country in the world.

Capital City:	Manila
Important Cities:	Quezon City, Davao City, Cebu City
Population:	101,833,938 (July 2011)
Official Languages:	Filipino and English
National Holiday:	Independence Day (June 12)
Religions:	Christian (92.5%), Muslim (5%), Other (2.5%)
Major Industries:	farming, fishing, manufacturing, mining, services
Natural Resources:	oil, natural gas, iron ore, copper, gold, nickel, limestone, phosphates
Manufactured Products:	electronics, clothing, footwear, medicine, chemicals, food products, oil products
Farm Products:	sugarcane, coconuts, rice, corn, bananas, cassava, pineapples, mangoes, pork, beef, fish
Unit of Money:	Philippine peso; the peso is divided into 100 centavos.

Glossary

ancestors—relatives who lived long ago

archipelago—a group of islands

Catholic—members of the Roman Catholic Church; Roman Catholics are Christian.

coral reefs—underwater structures off coasts; coral reefs are made of the skeletons of animals called corals.

fertile—supports growth

lava—hot, melted rock that flows out of an active volcano

minerals—elements found in nature; iron ore, copper, and zinc are examples of minerals.

monument—a structure built to remember and honor an important person or event

mountaineering—the sport of climbing mountains

native—originally from a specific place

natural resources—materials in the earth that are taken out and used to make products or fuel

Pacific Ring of Fire—an area in the shape of a ring around the edge of the Pacific Ocean; Earth's crust moves a lot in this area, causing earthquakes and volcanic eruptions in many countries that lie on the ring.

refine—to remove unwanted parts of a material; oil workers refine oil to make gasoline and other products.

revolution—an uprising of people who change the form of their country's government

service jobs—jobs that perform tasks for people or businesses

tropical rain forests—thick, green forests that lie in the hot and wet areas near the equator; it rains about 200 days each year in many tropical rain forests.

tsunamis—powerful waves caused by underwater earthquakes

vocational school—a school that teaches students how to do specific jobs

volcanoes—holes in the earth; when a volcano erupts, hot, melted rock called lava shoots out.

To Learn More

AT THE LIBRARY

de la Paz , Myrna J. *Abadeha: The Philippine Cinderella.* Auburn, Calif.: Shen's Books, 2001.

Gray, Shirley W. *The Philippines.* New York, N.Y.: Children's Press, 2003.

Oleksy, Walter. *The Philippines.* New York, N.Y.: Children's Press, 2000.

ON THE WEB

Learning more about the Philippines is as easy as 1, 2, 3.

1. Go to www.factsurfer.com.

2. Enter "the Philippines" into the search box.

3. Click the "Surf" button and you will see a list of related Web sites.

With factsurfer.com, finding more information is just a click away.

Index

activities, 20, 21
capital (see Manila)
daily life, 14-15
education, 16-17
food, 22-23
holidays, 24-25, 26
housing, 14-15
Independence Day, 24, 25
jeepneys, 15
landscape, 6-9
languages, 12, 13
location, 4-5
Luzon, 4, 5, 8, 13
Manila, 4, 5, 14, 27
Mindanao, 4, 5, 6
Mount Apo, 6
Mount Mayon, 9
National Heroes' Day, 25
Pacific Ring of Fire, 8-9
peoples, 13
Quezon City, 14
Rizal, José, 26, 27
Rizal Park, 26-27
sports, 20, 21
transportation, 14, 15
Visayas, 4, 5
wildlife, 10-11
working, 18-19

The images in this book are reproduced through the courtesy of: Jurgen Freund / NPL / Minden Pictures, front cover; Maisei Raman, front cover (flag), p. 28; Maggie Rosier, pp. 4-5; Mark Edwards / Photolibrary, p. 6 (small); Juan Martinez, pp. 6-7, 10-11, 12, 19 (right), 23 (right); StockTrek / Photolibrary, p. 8; Per-Andre Hoffman / Alamy, p. 9; Joe Belanger, p. 11 (top); Edwin Verin, p. 11 (middle & bottom); Neil McAllister / Alamy, p. 14; David Noble / Alamy, p. 15; Ron Giling / Photolibrary, pp. 16-17; Picture Press / Alamy, p. 18; Stuart Westmorland / Alamy, p. 19 (left); Mario Babiera / Alamy, pp. 20, 22; Marc F. Henning / Alamy, p. 21; Monkey Business Images, p. 23 (left); Romeo Gacad / Getty Images, p. 24; Tony Magdaraog, pp. 25, 27 (small), 29 (bill & coin); Laurie Noble / Getty Images, pp. 26-27.